Let's Go!

Plane Rides

By Pamela Walker

Welcome
Books

SCHOLASTIC INC.

New York   Toronto   London   Auckland   Sydney
Mexico City   New Delhi   Hong Kong   Buenos Aires

Special thanks to American Airlines

Photo Credits: Cover, pp. 5, 7, 9, 11, 19, 21 by Thaddeus Harden; pp. 13, 15, 17 © Index Stock Imagery

Contributing Editor: Mark Beyer
Book Design: MaryJane Wojciechowski

ISBN 0-516-23877-9

15 14 13 12 11   11/0

Printed in China.   62

First Scholastic printing, May 2002

Contents

I'm at the **airport** with my dad.

We are going on a plane ride.

The **pilot** shows me where he sits to fly the plane.

This room is called the **cockpit**.

It's at the front of the plane.

Our tickets tell us where to sit.

I like to sit next to the window.

9

Now it is time to buckle our **seat belts**.

My dad asks, "Are you ready for our plane ride?"

I say, "Yes!"

11

I hear the engines start up.

The plane moves toward the **runway**.

We are getting ready to **take off**.

The plane is going very fast.

We leave the ground!

We are going up into the air.

We are flying!

23R->

15

I look down and see tiny houses and roads.

The cars and trucks look like toys.

We eat lunch on this plane ride.

I get a sandwich and milk.

The plane lands.

The pilot says good-bye to us.

I can't wait for my next plane ride.

New Words

airport (**air**-port) a place where planes take off and land

cockpit (**cok**-pit) the room where a pilot sits and steers the plane

pilot (**py**-lit) the person who flies the plane

runway (**run**-way) the long road from which the plane takes off

seat belts (**seet beltz**) belts that lock around your waist when in a seat

take off (**tayk** off) when a plane lifts off the ground and begins to fly

To Find Out More

Web Sites
Knowble
http://www.knowble.com
Check out the airport section to see what it's like to fly a plane.

Off to a Flying Start
http://ltp.larc.nasa.gov/flyingstart/
Learn about the history of airplane flying, the parts of a plane, and how planes fly.

Index

About the Author
Pamela Walker lives in Brooklyn, New York. She takes a train to work every day, but enjoys all forms of transportation.

Reading Consultants

Kris Flynn, Coordinator, Small School District Literacy, The San Diego County Office of Education

Shelly Forys, Certified Reading Recovery Specialist, W.J. Zahnow Elementary School, Waterloo, IL

Peggy McNamara, Professor, Bank Street College of Education, Reading and Literacy Program